CLOTHING
in Different Places

Adrianna Morganelli

Crabtree Publishing Company
www.crabtreebooks.com

Learning About Our GLOBAL COMMUNITY

Author: Adrianna Morganelli

Publishing plan research and development: Reagan Miller

Substantive editor: Crystal Sikkens

Editor: Reagan Miller

Notes to educators: Shannon Welbourn

Proofreader and indexer: Janine Deschenes

Design: Samara Parent

Photo research: Samara Parent

Production coordinator and prepress technician: Samara Parent

Print coordinator: Margaret Amy Salter

Photographs:
istock: © Bartosz Hadyniak: p5 middle bottom, p9; © Bartosz Hadyniak: p8; © Bartosz Hadyniak: p13

Shutterstock: © Goran Bogicevic: front cover; © Anton Bielousov: title page; © meunierd: p4 bottom left, p20 bottom right; © Sarunyu L: p5 top left, p14; © Stephane Bidouze: p5 top right, p12; © FotograFFF p6; © Brendan Delany: p11 right

Superstock: Henry Georgi / All Canada Photos: p4 top right, p11 bottom left; p21 Photononstop: bottom

Wikimedia Commons: Public Domain: p19 right

All other images by Shutterstock

Front cover: These children in Peru are wearing traditional clothing.

Title page: Children wear traditional clothing at a First Nation Powwow in Canada.

Contents page: This schoolboy in Saudi Arabia wears traditional clothing.

Library and Archives Canada Cataloguing in Publication

Morganelli, Adrianna, 1979-, author
    Clothing in different places / Adrianna Morganelli.

(Learning about our global community)
Includes index.
Issued in print and electronic formats.
ISBN 978-0-7787-2010-2 (bound).--ISBN 978-0-7787-2016-4 (paperback).--ISBN 978-1-4271-1651-2 (pdf).--ISBN 978-1-4271-1645-1 (html)

    1. Clothing and dress--Juvenile literature. I. Title.

GT518.M66 2015   j391   C2015-903945-2
                                       C2015-903946-0

Library of Congress Cataloging-in-Publication Data

Morganelli, Adrianna, 1979-
 Clothing in different places / Adrianna Morganelli.
     pages cm. -- (Learning about our global community.)
 Includes index.
 ISBN 978-0-7787-2010-2 (reinforced library binding : alk. paper) --
ISBN 978-0-7787-2016-4 (pbk. : alk. paper) --
ISBN 978-1-4271-1651-2 (electronic pdf : alk. paper) --
ISBN 978-1-4271-1645-1 (electronic html : alk. paper)
 1. Clothing and dress--Cross-cultural studies--Juvenile literature. I. Title.

 GT518.M665 2016
 391--dc23

                    2015025714

Crabtree Publishing Company

www.crabtreebooks.com   1-800-387-7650

Printed in Canada/112015/EF20150911

Published in Canada
Crabtree Publishing
616 Welland Ave.
St. Catharines, Ontario
L2M 5V6

Published in the United States
Crabtree Publishing
PMB 59051
350 Fifth Avenue, 59th Floor
New York, New York 10118

Published in the United Kingdom
Crabtree Publishing
Maritime House
Basin Road North, Hove
BN41 1WR

Published in Australia
Crabtree Publishing
3 Charles Street
Coburg North
VIC 3058

Contents

Our Global Community

You play an important role. You help to make up your local **community**. A community is a place where people live, work, and play together. Your home and school are part of your local community. Together, all people around the world make up a global community. You are a part of this, too! We share Earth and its resources. In this way, the billions of people around the world are connected.

animal-skin clothing, Nunavut, Canada (page 11)

ARCTIC OCEAN

CANADA

NORTH AMERICA

U.S.A.

NORTH PACIFIC OCEAN

NORTH ATLANTIC OCEAN

MEXICO

COLOMBIA

PERU

SOUTH AMERICA

clothing from alpaca hair, Peru (page 20)

Different and alike

There are many ways in which people around the world are the same. There are also things that make us different and **unique**.

In this book, you will learn about the different kinds of clothes people wear in places around the world. Some of these pieces of clothing are shown on this map.

police officer in uniform, Qatar (page 14)

ARCTIC OCEAN

ASIA

EUROPE

FRANCE

school unforms, Japan (page 12)

NORTH PACIFIC OCEAN

JAPAN

AFRICA

INDIA

NIGERIA

ETHIOPIA

SOUTH ATLANTIC OCEAN

head covering worn in the Sahara Desert (page 9)

wedding dress, South Korea (page 18)

Sharing a Need

Along with shelter and food, clothing is a **basic need** all people share. A basic need is something people need to live. All people around the world wear clothing. People need clothing to protect their bodies from the heat or cold. However, people meet this need in different ways in different places.

Many people around the world wear similar clothing to people in North America. Some people, however, may wear different clothing for special **celebrations**.

Different clothes for different seasons

In some parts of the world the weather changes with the seasons. It may be cool and rainy during the spring and fall, sunny and warm during the summer, and snowy and cold during the winter. People living in these places wear different clothing for each season.

In the summer, people wear light clothes, such as shorts and T-shirts.

In the winter, people wear heavy coats, sweaters, and pants.

Hot Weather

Climate is the usual weather in a certain place. Climates can be cold or hot, wet or dry. People wear clothing to suit the climate where they live. People who live in hot climates wear long robes to protect their skin from the hot sun. Their clothing is made from light materials that let air flow through easily. This helps keep them cool.

Long, loose robes help keep people cool in Egypt's hot climate.

A *tagelmust* is also worn to protect a person's head from the burning sun.

Sand and sun

In hot, dry deserts, strong winds can pick up and blow large amounts of loose sand. People must wear clothing that prevents them from getting sand in their eyes and mouth. People living in the Sahara Desert in North Africa, wear a head covering called a *tagelmust*. A *tagelmust* is made of many layers of cotton cloth that cover the head and neck.

Cold Weather

In places with cold climates, the temperature is very cold for most of the year. Snow and ice cover much of the land. People living in these areas wear clothing that will keep them warm and dry. Many people wear layers of thick clothing. They also wear heavy coats with hoods called parkas.

This woman is wearing a parka. Parkas are long coats that go down to a person's knees.

Inuit clothing

The Inuit people who live in the northern polar regions were the first to create parkas. Traditional Inuit parkas were made of caribou or seal skin. They were sewn by hand and lined with fur. Mittens, pants, and boots were also made using animal skins and fur.

Many Inuit still wear traditional animal-skin clothing, such as this man from Nunavut, Canada.

Inuit clothing is also made with beautiful designs and patterns.

School Clothes

At some schools, children wear their everyday clothes. At other schools, all students wear the same kind of clothes. This is called a uniform. Uniforms can be different from school to school and place to place. At some schools in Japan, boys wear jackets called *gakurans* and girls wear pleated skirts.

These Japanese schoolchildren are on their way home from school.

Many schoolchildren in Burma wear white tops and green bottoms.

School colors

In some schools, children must wear clothing that matches their school's colors. Sometimes, the school's logo, or symbol, is sewn or printed onto the clothing. Some schools in China allow students to help design their uniforms.

Some people wear uniforms to their jobs. Their uniform helps other people recognize what kind of work they do. A person wearing a police officer or lifeguard uniform is someone who is safe to ask for help.

These police officers in Qatar are helping some boys that are lost.

Uniforms that protect

Some uniforms also protect the worker that is wearing it. Firefighters wear special uniforms to keep them safe in fires. Their clothing is made of **fire-resistant** material. This material protects the firefighter from the heat made by hot flames. It keeps the firefighter from getting burned.

A firefighter's uniform also includes a hard helmet which protects the firefighter's head.

Traditional Clothing

Culture is a way of life that a group of people share. Culture includes things such as language, religion, food, and art. Clothing is part of culture, too. Some clothing that is part of a person's culture is worn everyday. Other clothing is only worn on special occasions such as festivals, holidays, and ceremonies.

The *hijab* is a head covering that is part of the **Islamic** culture. Many **Muslim** girls and women wear a *hijab* when they are out in public.

Many graduation caps are square and contain a **tassel** that hangs off one side.

Graduation ceremonies

A graduation is a special ceremony that takes place when students finish high school, college, or university. Most graduates wear a cap and a long gown over their clothes. In some countries, graduates of college or university have colors on their gowns representing what they studied.

Marriage ceremonies

In many cultures, a wedding is a special ceremony in which a couple gets married. In many North American cultures, the bride wears a white wedding dress and a veil. A veil is a piece of fine material that covers the head or face. In other cultures, brides and grooms wear brightly colored outfits.

In some countries, such as India, grooms wear a long type of coat called a *sherwani*.

Brides in South Korea wear a dress called a *hanbok*.

Festivals

Many people wear traditional outfits to celebrate certain festivals or events. Scottish men and boys wear kilts for parades, dances, and **formal** events. A kilt is a skirt with a plaid pattern. A plaid pattern is made up of crisscrossing stripes.

Scottish people often wear kilts that feature their family's tartan, or plaid pattern.

Native people of North America celebrate their culture at festivals called powwows by wearing traditional clothing.

Materials

Clothing is made using different materials. In some places, people use the materials around them to make clothing. For example, people living in the mountains in Peru use hair from alpacas to make fabrics for clothing. Fabrics made from alpaca hair keep people very warm in the cold mountain climate.

alpaca

People in Peru earn money by selling the alpaca clothing they sew.

Soft silk

In countries such as Thailand, China, and India, silkworms are rasied to make silk. Silkworms are caterpillars that form a cocoon, or case, before they change into a butterfly. The threads of the silkworm's cocoon are used to make silk.

cocoon

silkworm

Silk is a very soft, smooth material.

Notes to Educators

Objective:
This title encourages readers to make global connections by understanding that even though people live in different kinds of climates and environments, people use clothing to meet the same basic need of comfort and protection.

Main Concepts Include:
- people choose different clothing to make them feel warmer or cooler, and to protect them from weather
- people wear clothes that suit their climate and environment

Discussion Prompts:
- Revisit the types of clothing described in the book. Connect each type of clothing to the climate and environment in which it is found. Ask readers how each type of clothing is suited for the climate or environment. How does each type of clothing compare to their own clothing? How is it the same? How is it different?

Activity Suggestions:
- Invite children to choose a specific country, area, or region, and design clothing that would be suitable for a boy and a girl. Have each child explain what materials they would use and how each relates to the climate or environment of their chosen area.
- Encourage children to add as much detail as possible about each of the pieces of clothing.
- Once completed, invite children to present their designs.
- Guide students by providing sentence starters such as:
- I designed clothing for _____ (country, region, area)
  OR
  - The climate is _____
  - The environment is _____ because they
  - The materials I chose for my design are _____ climate/environment. are suitable for a _____
- Encourage children to point out the different features they included in their designs.

Books

Adamson, Heather. *Clothes in Many Cultures*. Capstone Press, 2009.

Halstead, Rachel and Struan Reid. *Hands-on History Projects: Clothes.* Southwater, 2008.

Lewis, Clare. *Clothes Around the World.* Heinemann, 2014.

Websites

http://fashion-history.lovetoknow.com/clothing-around-world
Click on different links to learn in-depth about traditional items of clothing in different cultures and their materials, uses, and histories.

http://www.childrensuniversity.manchester.ac.uk/interactives/art&design/talkingtextiles/costume/
This interactive site that allows children to match traditional costumes with the country or continent they originated from.

http://angelibebe.com/2015/08/traditional-childrens-clothing-from-around-the-world/
Visit this site to explore children's traditional clothing around the world.

Glossary

celebrations [sel-uh-BREY-shuh n s] (noun) Special festivities or parties to mark an important day, person, or event

fire-resistant [FAHYUH R-ri-zis-tuh nt] (adjective) Not able to be burned

formal [FAWR-muh l] (adjective) Clothing designed for special occasions

Islamic [is-LAHM-ick] (noun) The religion practiced by followers called Muslims, based on the teachings of the prophet Muhammad

Muslim [MUHZ-lim] (adjective) Refers to the practicing of the religion of Islam

tassel [TAS-uh l] (noun) An ornament that hangs from clothing. Made of many long threads sewn together at one end.

unique [yoo-NEEK] (adjective) Something that is unlike anything else; on its own

A noun is a person, place, or thing. An adjective tells us what something is like.

Index

24